BRUNEL
AND THE VICTORIAN
ENGINEERS

Nigel Smith

WAYLAND

Great Victorians Series

Brunel and the Victorian Engineers
Darwin and the Victorian Scientists
Livingstone and the Victorian Explorers
Owen and the Victorian Reformers

Editor: Carron Brown
Cover designer: Jan Sterling
Designer: Malcolm Walker, Kudos Design
Production controller: Simon Eaton

First published in 1997 by
Wayland Publishers Limited
61 Western Road, Hove
East Sussex, BN3 1JD, England

Copyright 1997 © Wayland Publishers Limited

Find Wayland on the internet at http://www.wayland.co.uk

British Library Cataloguing in Publication Data
  Smith, Nigel, 1947 –
  Brunel and the Victorian Engineers. – (Great Victorians)
  1. Brunel, Isambard Kingdom, 1806–1859 – Juvenile
  literature
  2. Civil engineers – Great Britain – Juvenile literature
  3. Civil engineering – Great Britain – History –19th century
  – Juvenile literature
  1. Title II. Series
  624'.0922

ISBN 0 7502 2060 0

Typeset by Kudos Editorial and Design Services, England
Printed and bound by G. Canale & C.S.p.A in Turin, Italy

Cover (clockwise from left): The Clifton Suspension Bridge near Bristol; Isambard Kingdom Brunel; the SS *Great Britain*.

Picture Acknowledgements
The publishers would like to thank the following for allowing their pictures to be used in this book: Bridgeman Art Library, London /Agnew & Sons, London 12 (top); /City of Bristol Museum & Art Gallery 4; /Guildhall Art Gallery, Corporation of London 18; /Guildhall Library, Corporation of London 30, 43; /Institute of Mechanical Engineers, London 20 (bottom); /Maidstone Museum and Art Gallery, Kent 40; /Museum of British Transport 22; /Science Museum, London 11 (bottom), 33, 35; /Scottish National Portrait Gallery 11 (top); The British Transport Commission (Historical Records Section) 17; Mary Evans Picture Library 9 (top), 15 (top), 16, 20 (top), 21, 23, 24, 25 (top), 31 (top), 36, 37, 39; Brunel University Library 38; Hulton Getty 14 (top), 15 (bottom), 19, 26, 29 (top); Image Select 10 (top), 12 (bottom), /Ann Ronan Picture Library 25 (bottom), 31 (top), 41; National Portrait Gallery, London 35; Pictor *cover* [Clifton Suspension Bridge], 28 (bottom); Science Museum, London 42; SS *Great Britain* 6; Tony Stone; Wayland Picture Library *cover* [background], *cover* [Brunel], 8, 10 (bottom).

Although the publishers have made every effort to contact copyright owners, we apologise if anyone has been overlooked.

Contents

The Launch of SS *Great Britain*

At 6 a.m., on 19 July 1843, a train carrying two very important passengers left London's Paddington Station for Bristol. Queen Victoria's husband, Prince Albert, was on his way to the launch of a new ship, the SS *Great Britain*. The other, accompanying him, was the ship's builder and designer, Isambard Kingdom Brunel.

It was a great day for Brunel. The *Great Britain* was the largest ship ever built. It also had many amazing features that had never been used before in shipbuilding. The *Great Britain* was designed to be the safest and most comfortable ship that sailed the seas. It was the first steamship to be built of iron. The Great Western Railway line, on which the train ran to Bristol, was another of Brunel's great engineering achievements. On that historic day, Brunel must have felt very pleased with himself!

► *A huge crowd of excited onlookers cheered as the* Great Britain *sailed out of the dry dock, where she had been built, into Bristol Harbour.*

When they arrived at Temple Meads Station in Bristol, Brunel and Prince Albert were greeted by cheering crowds and a military band. Flags flew on all the buildings and shops, and businesses closed as people flocked to the riverside. A great banquet took place before the launch for six hundred important guests. Then Prince Albert broke a bottle of champagne against the ship's bows. The gates of the dry dock were opened and as the water rushed in, the huge bulk of the *Great Britain* floated out into the River Avon. Church bells rang, guns fired a salute and onlookers cheered and wept with excitement.

The *Great Britain* is to be launched,
With sailors bold well manned,
And thousands there to see the sight,
On the water and the land.
Oh, the largest steamship in the world
Great Britain it is she,
And she is launched July nineteen,
eighteen hundred and forty-three.

Part of a song written to celebrate the launch of the *Great Britain*.

Brunel must have been very proud as he watched his ship sail for the first time. At the age of thirty-seven, he had everything that mattered to him. His latest triumph was proof that he was the greatest engineer of his time. He had built railways, bridges and tunnels, and now he had built the most advanced ship. Brunel loved the importance and fame, as well as the money, that his success had brought him. He was a genius. His admirers called him 'Little Giant' because he was also short.

Some of Britain's greatest achievements in the nineteenth century were made through engineering. Engineers were the great heroes of the Industrial Revolution. Their work had made Britain a wealthy and successful nation. It seemed there would be no end to all the marvellous new inventions that were changing everyone's lives. The public were thrilled by the new railways that made the distance across Britain seem smaller. Now Brunel had built a steamship that could cross the Atlantic Ocean in just two weeks, the world began to seem smaller too.

But Brunel was never satisfied. He was always full of ideas and looking ahead to new projects. He had been like that ever since he was a child.

'These are indeed glorious times for engineers.'
James Nasmyth (1808–90), whose steam hammer was used in building Brunel's *Great Britain*.

► *Today, the* Great Britain *has been restored and lies permanently in the Great Western Dock in Bristol where she was built. Over 200,000 people visit the ship each year.*

Chapter One

∾ The Industrial ∾ Revolution

Britain was the world's first industrial nation. From the 1750s, huge changes took place in the way that goods were manufactured, as well as in transport and in just about every aspect of people's lives. The Industrial Revolution changed Britain completely.

Machines began to replace people in industries where previously everything had been made at home by hand. For the first time, all kinds of goods were mass-produced in factories. New factory towns such as Manchester and Birmingham rapidly grew into large cities. The steam-engine, factories, railways and canals all had a huge

Growth of Industrial Towns

	1801	1851
Birmingham	71,000	233,000
Bristol	61,000	137,000
Cardiff	2,000	18,000
Glasgow	77,000	345,000
Liverpool	82,000	376,000
Manchester	75,000	303,000
Portsmouth	33,000	72,000

▶ *Manchester became a great industrial city, with huge factories surrounded by overcrowded slum housing where the factory workers lived.*

impact on everyone. Industry soon became more important than farming. In 1750, most Britons still lived and worked in the countryside. By 1850, most people were living in towns and cities.

The Industrial Revolution made Britain a very powerful nation. However, those working directly in factory workshops or in other parts of industry did not get much benefit from the factory system. Many skilled workers lost their jobs because of the new machines. Some of them, like the handloom weavers, fought back. Known as the Luddites, they attacked factories and smashed the new machines. But the Luddites could never stop the progress of industrial change.

▲ *Luddites used huge hammers to smash the factory machines that they hated so much. Many Luddites were arrested, and some were even executed for being destructive.*

▲ *Factory workers' homes were overcrowded and very unhealthy, with little fresh air.*

People could no longer earn a living spinning and weaving cloth in their homes. Men, women and children had to seek work in the new factories. They all had to work very long hours. Often they were bullied and beaten by harsh factory overseers determined to make them work as hard as possible. Children as young as five or six years old were sent to work in factories and coal mines. Factory workers had to live in overcrowded, cheap slum housing built close to the factories.

However, businessmen and clever inventors had a chance to become very rich and important with the Industrial Revolution. Without a constant stream of new inventions, the Industrial Revolution would not have happened. The inventors' ambitions and ideas made progress possible, and helped turn Britain into a modern nation.

'Everything was new and strange to me … a few hundred yards brought us to a large trap door … This was to be my abiding place for the next twelve or thirteen hours, and my father set to work to make a trapper's hole behind the props, in which I might sit safely and comfortably.'

George Parkinson remembered his first day working in a coal mine at nine years old, in 1837. During the Industrial Revolution, very young children were employed to work long hours in mines and factories.

The most important invention of all was the steam-engine. It provided the power to drive the new machinery. No one can be sure who built the first steam-engine. People had known for a long time that steam could generate the power to move things. In 1712, Thomas Newcomen built a steam-engine to pump water out of coal mines. But it was James Watt who improved the steam-engine so that it could be used to drive factory machinery.

Watt worked at Glasgow University, making scientific instruments. One day he was asked to repair a working model of a Newcomen steam-engine. After Watt had studied the engine, he knew he could build a better one. Watt's engines were more powerful than Newcomen's and only used a quarter of the fuel that the older engines used. In 1775, Watt joined forces with a businessman called Matthew Boulton. Over the next few years, Watt and Boulton built and sold hundreds of steam-engines.

James Watt became extremely famous. His steam-engines made factory mass-production possible. When he died, because of his importance, James Watt was buried at Westminster Abbey in London.

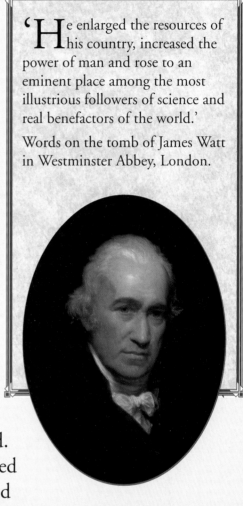

'He enlarged the resources of his country, increased the power of man and rose to an eminent place among the most illustrious followers of science and real benefactors of the world.'

Words on the tomb of James Watt in Westminster Abbey, London.

▶ *Watt's rotary engine was used to drive factory machinery.*

Iron was very important for the Industrial Revolution. It was needed in large quantities to build steam-engines, machinery, tools and household objects. The Darby family in Coalbrookdale, in Staffordshire, found new ways of producing iron as well as many new uses for it.

In 1709, Abraham Darby had begun to make iron using coke made from coal. It was the first time it had been done. Until then, charcoal, which comes from wood, had been used. Supplies of wood were running out. Using coke made it possible to produce huge quantities of iron quite cheaply. During the Industrial Revolution, the ironworks at Coalbrookdale were the most important in the world. They made iron cylinders for steam-engines and iron rails for railway lines. They supplied the iron plates for the hull of Isambard Brunel's SS *Great Britain*. Between 1777 and 1781, Abraham Darby III built a great iron bridge across the River Severn. It was the first time a bridge had been built out of iron.

▲ *Abraham Darby III expanded his family's Coalbrookdale Iron Company. He is best remembered for building the world's first cast-iron bridge.*

With the Industrial Revolution, there had to be a revolution in transport. It was a big problem moving raw materials such as coal and iron on the poor dirt-track roads of the eighteenth century. Factory owners demanded an easy, cheap way to transport their goods. New turnpike roads were built. People paid tolls (fees) to use them. Road engineers, such as John Metcalfe, John McAdam and Thomas Telford, pioneered new methods of road-building. McAdam invented the 'macadamizing' system of road-making, which used broken stones to make a strong surface.

▲ *John McAdam, a Scottish road builder, built many turnpike roads. He developed a cheap and effective way of giving roads a hard surface that lasted.*

◀ *The famous bridge at Ironbridge across the River Severn near Telford, has become the symbol of the Industrial Revolution. Ironbridge was the world's most important iron-making area in the late eighteenth century.*

Telford built a new road, including several important bridges, from London to Holyhead in North Wales. It was the main route for travellers on their way to Ireland. One of the bridges, the Menai Bridge in Wales, was described at the time as a 'stupendous structure'. It still carries traffic today. Telford also built important roads in the north of Scotland, including over 2,000 km of road in the Highlands.

▲ *Thomas Telford was the greatest of all the road builders. He built and improved hundreds of kilometres of hard-wearing roads that could carry heavy, horse-drawn vehicles.*

The problem of moving bulky and heavy goods such as coal and iron was partly solved by building canals. James Brindley, the son of a farm worker, led the way in building a canal network of 540 km in total, that linked all the important cities and ports. When he died at the age of fifty-six, it was said that he had worn himself out by his hard work. But, until the coming of the railways, the canals were a very important means of transport.

▶ *Telford's greatest achievement was the Menai Bridge. The suspension bridge over the Menai Straits joined North Wales and the island of Anglesey. It was and still is important for travellers on their way to and from Ireland.*

Men such as Watt, McAdam, Darby, Telford and Brindley were vital in making industrial progress happen. As well as skill, they also had the determination to make their ideas successful. They had to overcome thousands of engineering problems. Without their inventions there would have been no Industrial Revolution. The great engineers of the nineteenth century, including George and Robert Stephenson and Isambard Brunel, learnt a great deal from the work of the earlier engineers.

'I was quite astonished at the vastness of the plan and the greatness of the style of execution … the whole seems to be the work of giants rather than the production of our pigmy race of beings.'

Josiah Wedgewood, who owned a great pottery factory, said these words when he saw one of Brindley's canals.

▲ *James Brindley built many successful canals. They were a very important form of transport before the railways.*

◄ *Brindley's aqueduct carried the Bridgewater Canal over the River Irwell. By 1800, a network of canals linked the industrial areas in the Midlands and the North of England.*

Chapter Two

～ Isambard ～ Kingdom Brunel

Isambard Brunel's parents, Marc and Sophia, met during the turmoil of the French Revolution. Marc Brunel was born in France in 1769 and served as a naval officer. He was a loyal supporter of the French king, Louis XVI. So when the French Revolution overthrew and eventually caused the king to be executed, Marc was forced to flee from France. He escaped to the USA and became an American citizen. However, just before he left France he fell in love with an English girl called Sophia Kingdom.

▼ *Sir Marc Brunel was an important engineer and inventor. He wanted his son to be an engineer as well.*

In the USA, Marc Brunel decided on a new career as a designer and engineer. One of his first projects was to design a new Capitol building in Washington. He based it on the magnificent Palace of Versailles in France. This was far too expensive for the Americans. Soon after this proposal, Marc was appointed New York's Chief Engineer. He designed houses, public buildings and a new type of gun factory. But all the time he was in New York, Marc's thoughts kept turning to Europe and Sophia. He was eager to help the British in their war against the armies of the French Revolution. He also wanted to ask Sophia to marry him.

Sophia Kingdom Brunel (1775–1855)

At the age of seventeen, Sophia Kingdom's parents sent her to France to learn the language. It was a dangerous time to be in France. The country was in the grip of the revolution against the king. There was a Reign of Terror as Revolutionary mobs attacked and executed anyone who they thought was a supporter of the king. When Britain declared war against France, Sophia was captured and put in prison at Gravelines, just a few miles across the Channel from Britain. She expected to be executed as an enemy of the French Revolution! Eventually, Sophia was allowed to return to Britain.

In 1799, Marc Brunel sailed for Britain. His mind was full of ideas for all kinds of inventions. Some were successful like his machine to produce 100,000 pulley blocks per year for the Royal Navy. But quite a few of his other ideas were failures. However, he did succeed in marrying Sophia. When it came to business matters, Marc was rather vague and absent-minded. At one point, the couple ran out of money. After a while, Marc and Sophia owed so much money that they were sent to prison for three months. It was a dreadful experience. For Sophia, it was her second time in prison.

By the time Marc and Sophia went to prison, their son, Isambard, born in 1806, was a teenager. His parents had sent him off to school in France. Perhaps it was fortunate that he was there whilst his parents were in prison. Isambard was a very talented and careful youngster. When he was very young, about six years old, he was determined to follow his father and become an engineer. After all the family's money troubles, Isambard's parents might have preferred him to follow a different career!

▲ *Sophia Kingdom Brunel lived long enough to see her first child and only son, Isambard, succeed as a great and respected engineer.*

The years of the first half of the nineteenth century were very exciting for engineers. It was a time of great change and rapid progress. Improvements in transport were very important at this time. Marc Brunel's ambition was to build a tunnel under the River Thames from Rotherhithe to Wapping. It would be the first tunnel to be built under water. Marc gained permission to build the Thames Tunnel and work started in 1825. A great deal of the early work on the tunnel was supervised by Isambard. Building the tunnel taught him many important lessons about engineering that he found valuable in later life.

Unfortunately, there were many accidents and work stopped altogether for several years. At last in 1843, the two ends of the tunnel were joined. Isambard Brunel's three-year-old son, Isambard III, was handed across the tunnel and became the first person in history to pass underneath the River Thames.

◄ *Marc Brunel's Thames Tunnel. For the first time, Londoners could travel under the River Thames. The tunnel is now part of the London Underground railway.*

► *In this 1857 photograph, Isambard Brunel is sitting in front of his great but ill-fated steamship, the* Great Eastern.

When Isambard was seventeen years old his father told him, 'You have a career open to you from which you must seize every opportunity'. Marc lived until he was eighty-one years old, long enough to enjoy his son's success.

Isambard was an ambitious and proud man. In the nineteenth century, engineers and inventors enjoyed the same fame, wealth and respect as today's television entertainers and sportspeople. Isambard was determined to be the most successful of all. He admitted that he felt very important. All he ever wanted to do was to invent and build things. They had to be bigger and more advanced than any other engineers' work. He was always looking for new challenges. Brunel wanted to lead the way for other engineers to follow. Sometimes, this made him a difficult man to work for. His motto was 'En Avant' which is French for 'Get Going'.

'My love of glory is so strong, even on a dark night, riding home, when I pass some unknown person who perhaps does not even look at me, I catch myself trying to look big on my little pony ... I often do the most silly, useless things to attract the attention of those I shall never see again.'

Isambard Brunel, writing in his diary on 19 October 1827.

Chapter Three

❧ Brunel and the ❧ Railway Builders

▲ *The success of Stephenson's* Rocket *proved that steam locomotion really worked.*

Railways were the greatest of all the engineering achievements of the nineteenth century. In 1830, the Liverpool to Manchester railway line, built by George Stephenson and his son Robert, opened the Railway Age. Their steam locomotive, *Rocket*, proved that a steam-engine on wheels could pull heavily loaded trains. Around 50,000 people cheered with excitement as the first train to travel the new railway line rolled out of Liverpool. Soon businessmen wanted to build railway lines all over Britain. Everyone wanted the railway to come to their town.

George Stephenson (1781–1848)

George Stephenson is called the 'father of the railways'. From an early age he was fascinated by steam-engines. Although he never went to school, he taught himself to read and write. Helped by his son Robert, he built the world's first successful railway line, the Stockton to Darlington line which opened in 1825. After the success of the Liverpool to Manchester railway line, they built many other lines and locomotives. There was a lot of competition between the Stephensons and Brunel. Some people thought that only George Stephenson knew how to build a railway.

In the port of Bristol, the tradesmen worried that because they did not have a railway they would lose trade to Liverpool. In 1833, they appointed Isambard Brunel to build a railway line from Bristol to London. He was paid £2,000 a year, which in Victorian times was a great deal of money. Brunel was only twenty-seven years old. Building the railway was a massive task. But he already had experience in building bridges as well as the Thames Tunnel. Brunel had closely studied the work of the Stephensons. He was impressed, but he thought that he could build an even better railway line.

Brunel made his way along the entire route between Bristol and London on horseback and on foot as he worked out how he would build the railway. He decided the line would be called the Great Western Railway (GWR). Calling it 'Great' helped to convince wealthy people that it would be exciting and profitable to invest their money in it.

Brunel employed many people to help him build the GWR. But he was in charge and kept a close eye on every part of the work. He was a tough boss to work for. Brunel demanded the best and was quick to tell people off if he thought they were letting him down.

'You are a cursed, lazy, inattentive, apathetic [bored] vagabond, and if you continue to neglect my instructions, and to show such infernal laziness, I shall send you about your business.'

Part of a letter that Brunel wrote to one of his employees.

► *Working with only shovels and pick-axes, the labourers, known as navvies, built Britain's railways.*

The Box Tunnel

'The contractors, being exposed to fierce competition, adopt the cheapest method of working, without any regard to the danger to the men … Life is now recklessly sacrificed: needless misery is inflicted; innocent women and children are unnecessarily made widows and orphans; and such evils must not be allowed to continue, even though it is profitable.'

The *Manchester Guardian*, in 1846.

Thousands of navvies were employed to build the railway line. Many of them came from Ireland where famine and poverty drove millions of people to look for work in other countries. The navvies lived in large camps that were moved along as the line was built. It was hard and often dangerous work. They worked up to 16 hours a day in all weathers, every day of the week. On pay days, the navvies terrified local people with their heavy drinking and wild behaviour. Parents sent their daughters away for safety until the navvies had gone! A navvy had to shovel about 20 tonnes of earth a day. With pick-axes, shovels and wheelbarrows, the navvies built 32,000 km of railway track between 1825 and 1880.

The toughest job for the navvies working on the GWR was building the Box Tunnel, near Bath. Thousands of men and horses took five years to build it. It is 3.5 km long and was the longest tunnel ever built at that time. Gunpowder was used to blast through the clay and rock. There were many accidents. By the time the tunnel was completed, more than a hundred navvies had been killed. Trains still use the Box Tunnel. If you travel on the GWR and pass through it, think of the men who lost their lives there.

▲ *Daniel Gooch, Brunel's chief assistant on the GWR.*

Brunel was quick to spot and encourage talented men like himself. His chief assistant, Daniel Gooch, was only twenty years old when Brunel employed him. By then, Gooch had already designed powerful railway locomotives. He realized that some of the locomotives that Brunel had ordered for the GWR were not good enough for the job. He spent long hours in the engine sheds at Swindon working on improvements. For twenty-seven years, Gooch was in charge of the locomotives that ran on the GWR. The success of the railway owed a great deal to him.

◀ *Brunel designed the entrance to the Box Tunnel. More than thirty million bricks were used and many lives were lost building the tunnel. Brunel complained that it took too long to complete.*

The Great Western Railway or The Pleasure of Travelling by Steam

Of all the great wonders that ever was known,
And some wonderful things have been known in this town,
This Great Western Railway will beat them all hollow,
And who ever first thought of it was a wonderful fellow.

My good friends, when the railroad is finished,
All coachmen and cattle will for ever be banished;
You ride up to London in two hours and a quarter,
With nothing to drive you but a kettle of hot water.

You can breakfast at home on toast, tea and butter,
And need not to put yourself all in a splutter;
You may travel to London and dine there at noon
And be home to your tea again the same afternoon.

What a beautiful sight it will be for to see,
A long string of carriages on the railway,
All loaded with passengers inside and out,
And moved by what comes from a tea-kettle's spout.

Verses from a Bristol street song, written around 1839.

▶ *Brunel's Paddington Station, with its great arches and glass roof, was the London terminus for the GWR.*

'We arrived yesterday morning, having come by the railroad from Windsor in half an hour, free from dust and crowd and heat, and I am quite charmed with it.'

Queen Victoria's words after she had travelled on the GWR.

Brunel decided that the GWR railway lines would be wider than other railway lines. The width of railway lines, called the gauge, had been fixed by George Stephenson in the 1820s at 1.55 m. He seems to have based this on the width of the horse-drawn wagons pulled along lines at coal mines. Brunel decided on a broad gauge of 2.2 m for the GWR. It seemed a sensible decision. Broad-gauge trains could carry more people and they did not sway about as much at high speeds. Many people think that Brunel was right.

But, after a lot of argument, the government decided to make 1.55 m the standard gauge that is still used today. Many years after Brunel's death in 1859, the GWR was converted in 1892 to the narrower gauge. Brunel would have been very disappointed.

Total Kilometres of Railway Lines Open

Year	km	Year	km
1831	225 km	1847	6,349 km
1835	544 km	1848	8,251 km
1840	2,411 km	1849	9,706 km
1845	3,928 km	1850	10,655 km
1846	4,886 km	1851	11,067 km

It took a remarkably short time to build the GWR. On the 30 June 1841, the first passenger train left Bristol for London's Paddington Station. The 243-km journey took 5.5 hours. Until then, the stagecoach took about 20 hours. Stagecoach travel was expensive and very uncomfortable. Railways were cheap and fast, and soon put the stagecoaches out of business.

The Electric Telegraph

Brunel was one of the first people to realize the value of the electric telegraph. Between 1838 and 1842, an electric telegraph line was built alongside the GWR line from Paddington Station to Slough, in Berkshire. Messages in code were sent along the line. The telegraph was the invention of William Cooke and Charles Wheatstone. At first there was not much interest. Then in 1845, a woman was murdered in Slough and her attacker was spotted catching the train to London. The telegraph was used to alert the police in London and the murderer was arrested as he got off the train. He was later hanged.

Long before the telephone was invented, people found out how useful the telegraph could be to send messages very quickly. Railway companies used it to send messages about the progress and any delays of their trains. By 1852, 6,437 km of telegraph lines were in use. Most of them were set up alongside railway lines.

▲ *Charles Wheatstone.*

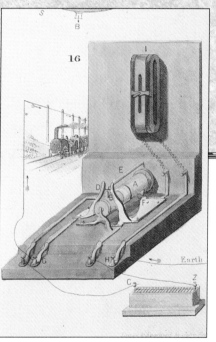

▶ *Wheatstone's telegraph machine was connected to telegraph lines running alongside the railway track.*

Brunel's success led to the building of many more railways. During the 1840s, everyone wanted to travel on the railway. Day trips to the seaside became popular. Businessmen travelled all over the country selling their products. Trained police could be sent from London to deal with disturbances anywhere in the country. Even royalty liked the trains. In 1842, Brunel accompanied Queen Victoria on her first train trip on the GWR. Her journey put the royal seal of approval on the railways.

The Victorians were very proud of their railways and the engineers who overcame so many problems to build them. The only problem that Brunel could not overcome was the awful coffee served at Swindon Station. He refused to drink it.

Chapter Four

∽ Brunel and the ∽ Bridge Builders

As well as being one of the great railway engineers, Brunel was also a master bridge builder. It was essential that railway engineers knew how to build bridges as these structures were needed to carry their railways.

It was the road engineers, such as Thomas Telford, in the late-eighteenth century, who first mastered the way to build strong bridges. In 1779, the Iron Bridge was built across the River Severn to replace small ferry boats. Afterwards, many more iron bridges were built, particularly to carry railways. Some rivers were too wide for the usual kind of bridge that was supported by pillars of stone or brick. In 1820, Sir Samuel Brown showed that it was possible to suspend a bridge using wrought-iron suspension chains. Both Thomas Telford and Isambard Brunel copied this technique.

Brunel faced a challenge when he designed a bridge to carry the GWR across the River Thames at Maidenhead. He had to make sure that there was enough room for the sailing barges, with their tall masts, to pass underneath. He sat on the riverside and drew up his design. The finished bridge has two of the largest and flattest arches ever built out of bricks. Some people feared it would collapse. However, it is still in use over 150 years later! As well as being an engineering success, it is considered to be a very beautiful bridge.

But it is the Clifton Suspension Bridge across the Avon Gorge at Bristol that is the best-known monument to Brunel's skill. It is one of the great feats of Victorian engineering, but most of the bridge was actually built after Brunel's death. In fact, it was not opened until thirty-four years after the first plans were drawn up.

Many wealthy people lived in Clifton near the city of Bristol. In the 1820s, a number of them decided they wanted a bridge built across the Avon Gorge so that they could travel easily into the country or the city. A competition was held to choose the best design. Brunel was determined to succeed. He knew that building the bridge would make him the leading engineer in Britain.

▼ *Telford's Menai Bridge is a very impressive suspension bridge. Brunel looked at it very closely before he designed the Clifton Bridge.*

Thomas Telford (1757–1834)

Telford was one of the greatest engineers ever. He was a successful road builder, but his greatest achievements were his bridges. His biggest engineering success was the bridge across the Menai Straits in Wales. It was the largest and strongest suspension bridge built at that time. Sixteen great chains held the roadway 30.5 m above the water. When it opened in 1826, the newspapers described it as a 'stupendous structure'. As well as bridges, Telford built roads and canals. He served as the first President of the Institute of Civil Engineers. In 1963, the new industrial town of Telford was named after him as a living memorial to one of Britain's greatest engineers. He is buried in Westminster Abbey, in London.

Brunel spent two days studying Telford's great suspension bridge across the Menai Straits in North Wales. Then, helped by his father, Marc, he drew up his design for the Clifton Suspension Bridge.

Out of twenty-two designs for the Clifton Bridge, only four were considered practical, including Brunel's design. Following his success with the Menai Bridge, Thomas Telford was asked to judge the designs. He rejected all of them. He thought that Brunel's plan was unsafe. A new competition was held. This time Telford put in his own design, but the great bridge builder's plan was not good enough. In the end, Brunel's design proved the best and he was given the job of building the bridge.

▼ *The magnificent Clifton Suspension Bridge is a spectacular monument to Brunel.*

Brunel called the Clifton Bridge his 'first child'. Yet he did not live long enough to see it finished. Work on the bridge went on and off for thirteen years. Then, with just the towers standing on each side of the gorge, work on it stopped altogether in 1843. There was not enough money to finish it. By this time, Brunel was busy building railways and steamships. Some Bristol people called for the towers to be torn down and for the planned bridge to be abandoned.

After Brunel's death in 1859, some of his friends decided that the bridge should be completed as a tribute to his life as an engineer. The Clifton Bridge finally opened in December 1864. Since then it has been used by millions of vehicles, from the horse-drawn carriages of the nineteenth century to modern motor cars. Because it was finished after his death, it is not really all Brunel's work. But although he built many other bridges, Brunel is remembered most for the Clifton Suspension Bridge that he never saw completed.

▲ *The opening of the Clifton Suspension Bridge in 1864. It is sad that Brunel did not live long enough to see his great design completed.*

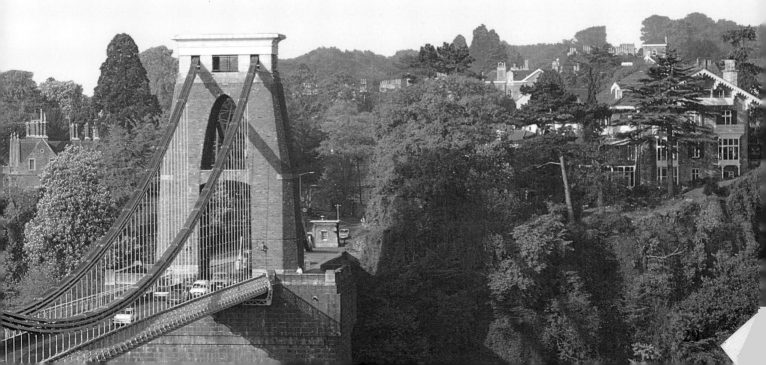

Chapter Five

∾ Brunel and ∾ the Steamships

Having made his reputation as an engineer building railways and bridges, Brunel turned his attention to steamships. His ambition was to extend the GWR journey all the way to New York 'by means of a steamboat to go from Bristol'. Brunel's work on steamships led to the building of great ocean liners. For nearly one hundred years, until air travel replaced them, these ships were the only way to travel from Europe to the rest of the world.

Ships were very important to British trade and power. The Industrial Revolution depended on raw materials such as cotton from the USA. Ships carried goods made in British factories to be sold in other countries. Merchants and settlers, supported by the Royal Navy, created a vast British Empire with colonies in every part of the world. New countries including Australia, Canada and the USA were growing up and attracting colonists to settle there.

▼ *The first successful steamship, the* Charlotte Dundas, *sailed on the River Clyde in 1802.*

Robert Fulton (1765–1815)

The USA's first successful steamboat, *Clermont*, built by Robert Fulton, began sailing on the Hudson River in August 1807. Her engine was built in Britain. Fulton wrote that the *Clermont* could overtake moving sailing boats as 'if they were at anchor'. Fulton had been an artist and for a time had lived in Britain working as a portrait painter. But he became so fascinated with machinery and ships that he gave up art and became an engineer.

Fulton built the first submarine, *Nautilus,* in France to fight against the British during the Napoleonic Wars. Perhaps, fortunately, it was never used. The success of the *Clermont* led him to build many more steamships. Soon, the USA's great rivers, such as the Missouri and Mississippi, were busy with steamships.

In 1800, all ships were made of wood and driven by sails. Then in 1802, William Symington, an English engineer, tried out an improved version of Watt's steam-engine on a boat, the *Charlotte Dundas*. In 1812, the *Comet*, built by Henry Bell, started the first passenger steamboat service, on the River Clyde in Scotland.

▲ *Robert Fulton's steamship,* Clermont, *operated the world's first regular steamship service between New York and Albany on the Hudson River, a distance of 240 km.*

Early steamships had huge paddles on either side. Their engines often broke down so the ships also had to be equipped with sails. Most people thought that steamships could only be used on rivers or for short sea journeys. It seemed impossible that a steamship could ever make the long journey across the Atlantic Ocean.

But in August 1833, a Canadian ship, the *Royal William*, did manage to cross the Atlantic Ocean powered entirely by steam. It took the ship twenty-five days. Her two great paddle wheels could only manage 20 revolutions a minute. Several times she had to stop altogether so that sea salt could be cleaned out of her boilers. Although the *Royal William* never crossed the Atlantic again, she had proved that a steamship could do it.

Brunel was excited by the *Royal William*'s voyage. It showed that his plan to make it possible for travellers to continue their journey to New York could work. Brunel set up the Great Western Steamship Company in 1836. In July 1837, there was great excitement in Bristol when Brunel launched his steamship, the *Great Western*. She was larger than any other ship and could carry 150 passengers and 57 crew.

Unfortunately, shortly before her maiden voyage, there was an explosion, and a fire broke out that nearly killed Brunel. He fell from a burning ladder and nearly drowned as water flooded into the boiler room. It took him several weeks to recover. News of the fire and Brunel's injuries spread quickly. Most of the passengers who had paid for the first trip were frightened and cancelled. When the ship sailed for New York there were only seven passengers on board.

▶ *Brunel's* Great Western *setting off for New York in 1838. She was the first great ocean liner.*

The *Great Western* crossed the Atlantic in just fifteen-and-a-half days. But she was beaten to New York by another steamship, the *Sirius,* which arrived a few hours ahead of the *Great Western*. The *Sirius* had actually set off four days earlier than the *Great Western* from Cork, in Ireland, which also made it a shorter crossing.

During the next eight years, the *Great Western* made sixty-seven Atlantic crossings. Her size, solid construction and reliable engines made her a very successful ship. But, unfortunately for her owners, she was expensive to run and did not make any profits.

Brunel tried to get the important contract for the *Great Western* to carry the Royal Mail between Britain and the USA. But the contract was given to an American rival, Samuel Cunard, instead. It was a great blow to Brunel. But it helped the Cunard Line on the way to becoming the greatest of all transatlantic shipping companies.

Brunel set to work building a new ship which he hoped would make more money. It was to be different from other steamships in two important ways.

The early steamships had been built of wood. In 1787, John Wilkinson built an iron barge to prove that iron boats could float. Iron was stronger and lighter than wood. Brunel's ship, the *Great Britain*, was made of iron. Instead of paddle wheels, Brunel took a chance on a new invention, the screw propeller. Using iron and the propeller made the *Great Britain* stronger and faster than other ships. She was to carry 252 passengers in comfort as well as a crew of 130.

The *Great Britain* was the most advanced ship of her time. But a series of mishaps destroyed any chance of her owners making a profit. The worst accident was when she crashed at high speed straight on to an Irish beach. Fortunately, no one was injured, but the accident ruined the Great Western Steamship Company.

▼ *The* Great Britain *marooned on the beach at Dundram Bay in Ireland.*

John 'Iron-Mad' Wilkinson (1728–1808)

John Wilkinson was always looking for new uses for iron. It was good for his business because he owned two ironworks. He made a lot of money from selling gun parts used in the war between Britain and her American colonies (1775–83). James Watt gave Wilkinson the job of making almost all the cylinders for his steam-engines. In 1788, Wilkinson supplied 64 km of cast-iron pipes for Paris's water supply. He earned the nickname 'Iron-mad'. When people said that an iron boat would sink, he built one to prove them wrong. After his death, he was buried in an iron coffin.

Eventually, the *Great Britain* was repaired. She made many voyages carrying emigrants to Australia to start new lives. The hull was so well built that the ship has survived until the present day as proof of Brunel's skill. Today, she rests in the same Bristol dry dock where she was built 150 years ago.

For a time, Brunel thought about retiring to a villa overlooking the sea at Torquay. If he had done so then he might have lived longer. But Brunel was always thinking of new projects. He decided he would construct an even bigger ship. It was to be far larger than any ship ever built. From the start he called it the 'Great Ship'.

'We have indeed been in fearful peril … Oh! I cannot tell you of the anguish of that night! The sea broke over the ship, the waves struck her like thunder claps. There was the throwing overboard of coal, the cries of children, the groans of women, the blue lights, the signal guns, even the tears of men and, amidst all, the Voice of Prayer, and this for long dark hours …'

The words of one of the terrified passengers when the *Great Britain* crashed.

▲ *The* Great Eastern *under construction at Millwall on the Isle of Dogs in London.*

Trade between Britain, India and Australia was very important and growing fast. Brunel designed a huge ship, the *Great Eastern*, that could carry over 6,000 tonnes of cargo and 4,000 passengers. It took nearly four years to build. As with all his projects, Brunel kept a close eye on every part of the ship's construction. Many problems had to be overcome. The cost was far more than had been expected and the shipyard went bankrupt. Brunel had to raise more money from the *Great Eastern*'s investors.

Once she was finished, the huge ship was difficult to launch. For more than ten weeks the shipbuilders struggled to get her into the water. By the time the *Great Eastern* was completed, Brunel was totally exhausted. On 5 September 1859, he saw the engine trials completed on his great ship. When he got home that evening, he collapsed and died ten days later.

Brunel's *Great Eastern* was a far too ambitious project. The ship had many accidents and never made any profits for her owners. She was simply too large. Perhaps her biggest achievement was in laying a telegraph cable across the Atlantic Ocean. This meant it took only a few minutes to send messages between London and New York. To send a letter took at least two or three weeks. The cable engineer was Daniel Gooch, Brunel's old assistant on the GWR.

For much of her life, the *Great Eastern* was no more than a floating fun-fair and exhibition centre. In the end, this magnificent ship was sold in 1867 for scrap metal and was broken up in the River Mersey.

'I have lost my oldest and best friend. He was the greatest of England's engineers, with the greatest originality of thought and power of execution, bold in his plans but right. The commercial world thought him extravagant; but though he was so, great things are not done by those who count the cost of every thought and act.'

When he heard of Brunel's death, Daniel Gooch, who had worked with him on the GWR, wrote these words in his diary.

◄ *Brunel, smoking a cigar, watched anxiously at the launch of the* Great Eastern. *It took several attempts to launch the giant ship.*

The *Great Eastern* had been an unlucky ship. It is said, although it might not be true, that she carried the body of a man. As the ship was broken up, it is said that workmen found the skeleton of a man who must have been trapped during the building of her hull!

Working on the *Great Eastern* is said to have killed Brunel. He would have been dreadfully disappointed that the ship was not successful, but it was still a great engineering achievement. People said that she had been 'born out of her time'. Many of Brunel's methods were later used by other shipbuilders.

▼ *The* Great Eastern *just before the final attempt to launch her. The ship was moved sideways into the River Thames.*

In the years after Brunel's death, hundreds of ocean liners and battleships were built by British shipbuilders. In 1900, Britain possessed the largest fleet of merchant ships as well as the world's most powerful navy. Thousands of emigrants from Europe were carried by steamship to their new lives in Australia and the USA. Until jet air travel replaced them, great ocean liners, such as the *Normandie, Queen Mary* and *Queen Elizabeth*, were the only way for people to travel between Europe and the rest of the world.

Isambard Brunel had been ahead of his time, but he had played a vital part in the success of British shipping.

▲ *Brunel never saw the* Great Eastern *at sea. She was a marvellous sight. The greatest ship of her time, she paved the way for the ocean liners of the twentieth century.*

Chapter Six

The Triumph of the Victorian Engineers

▲ *The Crystal Palace was built to house the Great Exhibition. Visitors to the exhibition had never seen a building made from so much glass before.*

In 1851, a remarkable exhibition was held in London. The 'Great Exhibition of Science and Industry of All Nations' was held to celebrate one hundred years of industrial progress. It was a wonderful chance to show off Britain as the leader in engineering and industry. Britain was known as the 'workshop of the world'. Inventions such as the railways and steam-driven machinery were slowly spreading to other countries. But they had started in Britain. Victorians were very proud of the success of the Industrial Revolution that had started one hundred years earlier.

Queen Victoria opened the Great Exhibition on 1 May 1851. Because of Isambard Brunel's importance as one of Britain's greatest engineers, he walked close to the front of the grand procession at the opening ceremony.

The Great Exhibition was held in a vast building made from iron and glass, called the Crystal Palace, in Hyde Park, London. It was designed by Joseph Paxton, who earned his living designing gardens and conservatories. Visitors were astonished by the beauty and size of the building. Within an iron framework, the building was covered with 300,000 panes of glass to give plenty of natural light to the Exhibition. Instead of cutting down the trees in the park, they were left standing inside the building. Brunel was very impressed. In some ways it was similar to his own design for Paddington Station, which still has a large glass roof. To the Victorians, the Crystal Palace was yet another achievement of the industrial age.

Inside the Great Exhibition, visitors gazed at the wonders of the era. Exhibits came from all over the world, but it was the British exhibits that thrilled and impressed everyone. Most of these were new inventions and machines from British industry. People crowded into the section displaying steam-engines. It was, after all, the steam-engine that had made the Industrial Revolution possible. More than sixty steam-driven machines were displayed, including a steam hammer, a riveting machine and a travelling crane. Visitors watched amazed as one machine churned out thousands of gummed envelopes.

▲ *Queen Victoria led the opening ceremony at the Great Exhibition.*

'Went to the machinery part, where we remained two hours … What used to be done by hand and used to take months doing is now accomplished in a few instants by beautiful machinery. We saw first the cotton machines from Oldham … We saw hydraulic machines, pumps, filtering machines of all kinds, machines for purifying sugar – in fact every conceivable invention.'

Queen Victoria's description of her visit to the Great Exhibition.

There were steam-driven weaving looms, printing machines and one machine that could mass-produce medals. Of course, the latest railway locomotives were on display as well as a model railway.

The Exhibition was a great celebration of Britain's industrial success and people loved it. During the 141 days that it was open, it attracted over six million visitors. Most of them travelled to London on the new railways. For many working-class people, it was their first ever train trip and their first visit to London. It must have been very exciting for the mill workers from Lancashire, the farm workers from Dorset and the miners from Newcastle as they set off for London.

Different admission charges kept the rich and poor apart. On some days, the cost was £1 which was then very expensive. This meant that wealthy people could enjoy the sights without being jostled by crowds. On other days, when the price was a shilling (5p) the exhibition was often packed out. These ordinary visitors were nicknamed the 'shilling folk'. The record number of visitors on a single day was 93,224!

By the end of the Great Exhibition, a large profit of £186,437 had been made. That was a vast sum of money in 1851. A great deal of the money was used to set up great London museums including the Victoria and Albert Museum and the Science Museum. People could not bear to lose the Crystal Palace. So it was carefully dismantled and rebuilt in South London. Sadly, this wonderful building burnt down in 1936.

▼ *The latest machinery was shown working in the Machine Hall at the Great Exhibition. In the nineteenth century, British engineers led the way with new inventions.*

Even Brunel could not have guessed what great inventions and progress would be made in the years after the Great Exhibition. Some of the children who were taken by their parents to the Crystal Palace lived long enough to see the arrival of the motor car, the telephone and, if they lived to be eighty years old, they might even have seen one of the first aeroplanes.

'Manufacturers have not only given their workpeople a holiday to visit the Exhibition, but have paid the expenses both of the trip and of their admission. We rejoice to see such examples of kind feeling.'
Illustrated London News,
28 June 1851.

Sir Joseph Bazalgette (1819–91)

In 1855, Bazalgette, an English engineer, started building London's first proper system of sewers. Raw sewage was no longer simply dumped into the River Thames. Pumping stations took the sewage out of London. Bazalgette's work greatly improved the cleanliness and health of Londoners.

Many of those who went to the Great Exhibition lived in dirty and unhealthy slum houses. At first, engineers were more interested in building great machines and ships than planning better living conditions, although, Brunel had designed 'model' housing for some of his railway workers.

People in the cities needed a clean water supply. Robert Thom, a Scottish engineer, showed how everyone could be supplied with clean water. By 1827, he had completed a proper water supply in Greenock in Scotland. His work helped to cut the number of deaths from diseases, such as cholera and typhoid, that were carried by dirty water.

One of the great achievements of the Victorians was to make Britain a healthier place to live in. Hundreds of kilometres of sewage pipes were built under cities. Clean water was pumped from new reservoirs.

None of this would have been possible without the engineers. A person living in 1860 could tell you that Paxton had designed the Crystal Palace and that Brunel had built the *Great Eastern*. Engineers were household names. But in the 1990s, can anyone tell us who planned the Channel Tunnel, the Severn Bridge or the new British Library building?

IMPORTANT DATES

1769 Birth of Marc Brunel.

1775 Birth of Sophia Kingdom.

1776 James Watt's steam-engine in use.

1779 Iron Bridge built at Coalbrookdale.

1787 Cast-iron barge launched.

1789 Beginning of the French Revolution.

1799 Marc Brunel marries Sophia.

1802 The first successful steamship, *Charlotte Dundas* launched.

1806 Isambard Kingdom Brunel born.

1811 Luddite riots start.

1814 Steam printing press used to print *The Times*.

1822 Isambard begins working with his father.

1825 Work begins on the Thames Tunnel.

1830 Stephenson's Liverpool and Manchester Railway opened. Brunel appointed to build the Clifton Suspension Bridge.

1833 Brunel appointed engineer to the Great Western Railway. First Factory Act to restrict the working hours of women and children.

1836 Brunel marries Mary Horsley.

1837 Victoria becomes queen. Electric telegraph developed.

1838 Steamship *Great Western* launched.

1841 Great Western Railway completed.

1843 Thames Tunnel opens.

1844 Start of railway 'mania'.

1845 Maiden voyage of the *Great Britain*.

1848 Brunel builds a railway in Devon.

1849 Death of Marc Brunel.

1851 The Great Exhibition held in the Crystal Palace in London.

1857 Steam power used to generate electric light.

1858 Launch of the *Great Eastern*.

1859 Death of Isambard Brunel.

1864 Brunel's Clifton Suspension Bridge completed.

1866 Transatlantic cable laid.

GLOSSARY

Bankrupt A person who owes a great deal of money and is unable to pay it.

Banquet A special meal held to celebrate an important occasion.

Civil engineer A person who designs and builds roads, tunnels, bridges and large buildings.

Coke A fuel made from coal that is used to make metals such as iron.

Colonies Countries that are owned and controlled by another country.

Contract A written agreement between two or more people where something is agreed to be carried out.

Cylinder Part of the engine that a piston moves in.

Electric telegraph A system of sending messages along a line using electrical impulses.

Emigrants People who leave their country and go to live in another country.

Engineer A person who has studied how to design and build machines, engines, roads and railways.

Exhibit To put on show for people to look at.

Factory system Goods made by machines in factories.

French Revolution The violent uprising in 1789 in France that ended the power of the royal family and set up the French Republic [1792].

Handloom weavers Men who operated hand-powered weaving machines.

Hydraulic machines Machines operated by the movement of water or oil under pressure.

Industrial Revolution The period between 1750 and 1850 when there were rapid changes in industry. This was made possible by the invention of new machines and the steam-engine.

Invest People who put money into a business. These are called investors.

Journal A kind of diary where someone writes down everything they do each day.

Launch To move a ship into water for the first time.

Locomotive A steam-driven engine that is used to move trains along railway tracks.

Luddites Skilled craftspeople who smashed the new factory machines that were destroying their jobs.

Machine A piece of equipment driven by an engine powered by steam, or nowadays by electricity or petrol.

Maiden voyage The first voyage of a ship.

Manufacturers The owners of the factories that make various products.

Merchant A person who buys and sells large quantities of goods.

Merchant ship A ship that carries cargo or passengers.

Navvies Labourers who build canals, roads and railways.

Raw materials Things such as timber or coal that are used to make products.

Reservoir A natural or man-made lake where water is stored.

Sanitation Trying to improve people's living conditions by making sure that everyone has proper sewerage and clean water supplies. Proper sanitation helps to prevent disease.

Slum houses Very poor houses which are over-crowded, dirty and often do not have toilets or a proper water supply.

Stagecoach A horse-drawn carriage.

Suspend To hold something from above.

Turnpike Where gates are placed across a road to stop traffic from passing until a toll (fee) has been paid.

Vagabond Someone who is lazy, or a beggar who has no proper home.

Victorian Relating to the reign of Queen Victoria (1837–1901).

FURTHER INFORMATION

Books to Read

Nigel Smith, *History Makers of the Industrial Revolution*, (Wayland, 1995).
Nigel Smith, *The Industrial Revolution*, (Wayland, 1990).
Richard Tames, *Isambard Kingdom Brunel*, (Shire Publications 1972, reprinted 1992).
Adrian Vaughan, *Isambard Kingdom Brunel*, (John Murray, 1991).

Places to Visit

The British Engineerium, off Nevill Road, Hove, East Sussex BN3 7QA Tel: 01273 559583
This museum is situated within Brighton's 1866 water pumping station. It houses many models of steam models, including one of the first locomotives designed by George Stephenson.

Brunel Engine House, Tunnel Road, Rotherhithe Street, Rotherhithe, London, SE16 4LF.
Tel: 0181 318 2489. Part of the tunnel built by Marc and Isambard Brunel. There is a small museum.

Clifton Suspension Bridge, Avon Gorge, Bristol. This great bridge still carries traffic and pedestrians.

Great Western Railway Museum, Farringdon Road, Swindon, Wiltshire. Tel: 01793 493189.
This museum is devoted to relics of the GWR with locomotives and a Brunel Room which includes his drawing board.

Ironbridge Gorge Museum, Ironbridge, Telford, Shropshire. Tel: 01952 433522
Museum displays remains of the Industrial Revolution including the ironworks that made plates for the SS *Great Britain* and a recreation of a nineteenth-century industrial village.

Maidenhead Railway Bridge, Maidenhead, Berkshire. Brunel's famous bridge can be best seen from the Thames towpath on the downstream side.

Paddington Station, London. This station built by Brunel is still the terminus for trains from Bristol and Wales. There is an impressive statue of Brunel.

Science Museum, Exhibition Road, London SW7 2DD. Tel: 0171 938 8000. Many exhibits from the Industrial Revolution including Stephenson's *Rocket* and models of Brunel's ships.

SS *Great Britain*, Great Western Dock, Gasferry Road, Bristol BS1 6TY. Tel: 0117 926 0680.
Brunel's magnificent ship has been restored in the dock where she was built.

Temple Meads Station, Bristol. Impressive station buildings designed by Brunel.

INDEX